The Berlin Olympics

THE BERLIN OLYMPICS, 1936

When the National Socialists (the Nazis), led by Adolf Hitler, took over Germany in 1933, the Olympic Games of 1936 were already scheduled to be held in Berlin. Joseph Goebbels, German propaganda minister, convinced a doubting Hitler that the Olympics would be a great opportunity to impress the world. The Germans thereupon built in Berlin a huge stadium seating over 100,000 people, surrounded by a sports complex spread over 356 acres. A fine Olympic Village was constructed to house most of the contestants, and Berlin was cleaned and decorated until the capital sparkled. People coming from all over the world were much impressed with the city and the sports facilities. Track and field were the most popular events; they were held in the stadium, the seats were jammed, and Hitler was usually there. The Nazis, who believed that "Nordic" Germans should not be forced to compete against inferior "non-Aryans," found to their chagrin that American blacks were the stars of these events. Foremost was Jesse Owens, who won four gold medals. On two occasions Hitler left early, apparently to avoid victory ceremonies for black Americans. When the final scores for all sports were in, Germany had more points than any other country because it dominated many of the lesser-known sports. The United States was second, but had swept the prestigious track and field events, largely because of its black athletes. Hitler's propaganda had been partly successful, but the black Americans had made his racial theories of "Nordic" supremacy look very foolish.

PRINCIPALS

ADOLF HITLER (1889–1945), chancellor and dictator of Nazi Germany.

JESSE OWENS (1913–), black star of track and field events, winner of four gold medals.

HELEN STEPHENS (1918–), star of women's events; set 100-meter record not broken until 1960.

JOSEPH GOEBBELS (1897–1945), Nazi propaganda minister who convinced Hitler to hold the 1936 Olympic Games.

LUTZ LONG (–1943), German broad jumper who competed with Owens, but became his friend.

ELEANOR HOLM JARRETT (1914–), swimming champion disqualified by U.S. Olympic officials in a controversial decision made before the games began.

CORNELIUS JOHNSON (1916–1946), University of California black student, winner of the high jump.

JOHN WOODRUFF (1915–), University of Pittsburgh black freshman, winner of the 800-meter run.

RALPH METCALFE (1912–), black sprinter second only to Owens; member of the winning 400-meter relay team.

JACK LOVELOCK (1910–1949), brilliant winner of the 1,500-meter run; a New Zealander studying medicine in London, popular hero of the Olympics with Owens and Stephens.

THE BERLIN OLYMPICS

1936
Black American Athletes Counter Nazi Propaganda

By James P. Barry

A World Focus Book

FRANKLIN WATTS, INC.
NEW YORK | 1975

Photographs courtesy of: German Information Center: 24; Landesbildstelle: 13; The Library of Congress: x, 66; Schirner: 22 (above and below), 27 (above and below), 28, 36, 41 (above and below), 42, 49, 50, 63, 71; United Press International: 21 (below), 44, 58; U.S. Information Agency in the National Archives: 53 (below); World War II Collection of Seized Enemy Records in the National Archives: frontispiece, 4, 7, 10, 16, 21 (above), 33, 53 (above).

Frontispiece photograph: A dirigible's-eye view of the Olympic Stadium, Berlin, 1936

Cover design by Nicholas Krenitsky

Library of Congress Cataloging in Publication Data

Barry, James P

The Berlin Olympics, 1936: Black American athletes counter Nazi propaganda.

(A World focus book)

Bibliography: p.

Includes index.

SUMMARY: Discusses the background and significance of the 1936 Olympic Games in Berlin, emphasizing the effect of the black American athletes' victories on Hitler's theories of Nordic supremacy.

1. Olympic Games, Berlin, 1936–Juvenile literature. 2. Negro athletes–Juvenile literature. [1. Olympic Games, Berlin, 1936. 2. Negro athletes] I. Title.

GV722 1936.B3 796.4'8 74–28173

ISBN 0–531–01090–2

Printed in the United States of America
5 4 3 2 1

Contents

The Berlin Olympics

The 1936 Olympic Games open

Berlin,
August 1, 1936

Overhead, under gray clouds, circled the big dirigible *Hindenburg,* trailing the Olympic flag. A huge bell in a tower just outside the stadium rang at thirty-second intervals. As the last sound and echoes of the bell died slowly, the orchestra of one hundred musicians, conducted by the famous composer Richard Strauss, struck up a march. The parade of the athletes began.

The first of the fifty teams to enter through the gate at the western end of the gray-stone stadium was from Greece; the Greeks had originated the Olympic Games in ancient times, and for that reason were now given the position of honor. Then followed each country in alphabetical order except for the Germans, who, as hosts of these Olympic Games, marched last. Each team carried its national flag. The teams from two small countries, Costa Rica and Haiti, consisted of one man each, so that man also had to be the flag bearer. With the Swiss team, in addition to the flag bearer, marched a man who twirled and tossed a baton with a flag attached at one end.

The audience of 110,000 in the huge stadium watched closely while the teams marched along the dull-red cinder track that circled inside the stadium and then moved into position on the green field. As each team passed the reviewing stand, halfway along one side of the stadium, it saluted. In the stand were the international Olympic officials; but also in it were Adolf Hitler, chancellor and dictator of Germany, plus the king of Bulgaria and a number of princes from other countries.

The long-established Olympic salute was almost the same as the straight-armed Nazi salute. Thus, often it was not quite clear just who was being saluted, or how. When the Bulgarians dipped their flag to the cinders, marching with the stiff-legged goose step used by German troops on parade, and raised their arms in salute, the audience cheered loudly at this supposed compliment to Hitler. Most of the spectators were unaware that the salute was for the king of Bulgaria, who stood next to him.

The French gave a straight-armed salute, bringing cheers from the German spectators and lengthy arguments later as to just which salute it was. The salute of most Austrians was clearly a compliment to the Nazi leader and brought loud applause, though a few of the Austrian team pointedly held their arms out to the side so that their salutes would not be confused with those of the others. The British merely passed with eyes right; the crowd reacted with glum silence. Each team was preceded by its flag bearer, and nearly every one dipped its flag as it passed, until the second-to-last team appeared–that of the United States. As the American athletes passed with eyes right and held their hats over their hearts, the American flag was held high. As one account puts it, "the applause given the big American team was described as mild." In fact, the people in the stands, who were unaware that U.S. custom forbids the dipping of the national flag in salute, began to whistle–the European equivalent of a boo or a hiss.

But at that moment the German team, marching in perfect order, entered the field. Immediately the attention of nearly everyone present switched to it. The orchestra began to play a Nazi march. The vast crowd rose and stood at attention; most of them stretched out their arms in the Nazi salute. While the audience was thus occupied, the Americans moved without further incident to the formation in the center of the field.

After the Germans took their place on the field, there followed the broadcasting of a short recorded speech from the elderly and ailing Pierre de Coubertin, the Frenchman who had revived the Olympic Games in modern times; he was too ill to be present at Berlin. After that came a dull twenty-minute speech in person by the president of the German Olympic Committee. Finally Hitler, dressed in the brown uniform of a Nazi storm trooper, stepped forward to the microphone and declared crisply that the Games of Berlin were opened.

Massed trumpeters sounded a fanfare. Cannon outside the stadium began to fire a twenty-one-gun salute. Uniformed German sailors raised the Olympic flag on the main pole at the end of the field while other uniformed German sailors raised the national flags of the participating countries on the fifty smaller poles around the top of the stadium. Boys of the Hitler Youth, stationed at the edges of the field, opened cages to release twenty thousand white doves, which rose in a cloud over the stadium while a massed chorus of three thousand people sang an Olympic hymn composed by Richard Strauss.

As the chorus sang its last note, there appeared on the steps at the eastern gate of the Stadium a young man carrying a burning torch—the sacred flame, carried in relays by runners all the way from the altar at Olympia in Greece. For a moment this last runner, a slim, blond German, held the torch high in a dramatic gesture; then he ran quickly the length of the stadium, climbed easily up the steps to a platform above the western gate, and lighted the fire that was to burn there throughout the games. After that he was gone, leaving behind the Olympic fire and a lingering wisp of smoke from his torch.

The color bearers of the fifty teams then carried their flags forward into a half circle around a low platform, upon which the German weight-lifting champion stood while he read into a microphone the Olympic oath for all the athletes assembled there. Finally, after the flag bearers returned to their teams, a thin old man stepped forward from the Greek team; he was

Spiridon Loues, winner of the marathon at the first modern Olympic Games in 1896. He was taken up to Hitler; and he presented the dictator with an olive branch—the ancient symbol of peace—brought from Olympia. It was an emotional scene, with tears running down the cheeks of the old man and Hitler himself visibly touched.

Hitler accepts an olive branch from Spiridon Loues

The International Scene

At the beginning of March, 1936, four months before the Berlin Olympics, Hitler sent a military force into the Rhineland, the German-French border area that had been made a demilitarized zone by the Treaty of Versailles at the end of World War I. The German generals fully expected that the much larger and better-equipped French army would promptly throw them out of the Rhineland again. Had this happened, Hitler's whole government would probably have collapsed; but the French army had become flabby in spirit since the end of the war and refused to act unless there was a full-scale French mobilization. The German force stayed where it was. As a result, Hitler was immeasurably strengthened, both within Germany and outside it.

In July of 1936, the month before the Olympics, the Spanish Civil War erupted. As the war progressed, Hitler dispatched nearly seventy thousand troops, together with arms and aircraft, to help General Francisco Franco, the Spanish Fascist leader. One of the German chancellor's major aims was to prolong the civil war, thus isolating Italy—who was also helping Franco—from its old friends Britain and France, and bringing the country under German influence. (This move by Hitler was largely responsible for the close association of Italy and Germany in what later became known as the Rome-Berlin Axis.) Because of the outbreak of war, the Spanish Olympic team returned home from Berlin before the games started.

Throughout the two weeks of these Olympic Games, head-

Olympic ceremonies in Berlin

lines and pictures of the games in the newspapers were overshadowed by headlines and pictures of the fighting in Spain. Sportswriter John Lardner commented midway through the games: "The most interesting event of the Olympic program is the race to see which country can get to Spain first with the biggest load of shells."

All of this time Hitler was looking forward to World War II. His planning came to a logical culmination in September, 1936, just after the Olympics were over, when he secretly placed General Hermann Göring in charge of a Four-Year Plan to prepare Germany for war. Or rather, as Göring himself put it to a group of industrialists and high officials: "We are already at war. All that is lacking is the actual shooting." (Within two years Germany moved into Austria and Czechoslovakia.)

But the foreigners who crowded into Berlin for the Olympics knew nothing of the coming Four-Year Plan, and both the Rhineland invasion and the German intervention in Spain seemed small matters to many of the visitors. For the duration of the Olympics the Nazis had taken down the anti-Jewish propaganda posters that normally were spread through the country, they had taken their traffic police out of military uniforms and put them in less formal costume, and they had scrubbed and painted and polished Berlin so that it was a showplace. Foreigners could buy German money at rates set especially low by the government, and meals and hotel rooms were kept artificially cheap by the government. There were special inspectors who checked shops, restaurants, and hotels to make certain that they held their prices at the lowest levels. Everything was done to convince foreigners that Germany was a peaceful and wonderful place; and as the white doves of peace flew upward during the Olympic opening ceremonies, many of the visitors were indeed convinced.

The Road to Berlin

Germany—economically weak and politically unsettled after its defeat at the end of World War I, demoralized by a brief civil war in 1918–19, plagued through the 1920s by hundreds of political assassinations and constant political upheaval—almost achieved stability during the prosperity of the late twenties, but then plunged into final chaos when the Great Depression began in 1929. By 1932 much of the labor force was out of work and the situation was rapidly deteriorating. There were riots in the streets of every large German city. Various political groups, ranging across the spectrum from Communists to right-wing nationalists, plotted, brawled, and tried in every possible way to turn events to their own advantage. One of the nationalist groups was headed by a spellbinding orator named Adolf Hitler, who was more adroit and less scrupulous than all the others; in January of 1933 Hitler became chancellor of Germany.

Within a year Hitler's party, the National Socialists (commonly known as the Nazis), had set up the whole apparatus of dictatorship, including one-party government and concentration camps, and the Nazi revolution was complete. A major feature of the Nazis' public activities had always been showmanship; in his early days, in the Munich beer halls where his movement got its start, Hitler saw to it that his ranting speeches were turned into colorful ceremonies by the use of banners, torchlight, and music. Now that he had the full resources of the nation at his disposal, his ceremonies became colossal productions. The early Nazi meetings at Nuremberg were political spectacles unlike anything else then known. Great masses of perfectly drilled people marched, sang, and cheered in specially

Hitler speaking in the streets in 1928

designed halls and stadiums, in response to commands given over specially designed loudspeakers; after dark there were torchlight parades in which thousands participated while searchlights stabbed vertically into the night and great bonfires burned along the horizon.

Many of the spectacles were framed in pagan terms, using old pre-Christian Nordic customs and deferring to old gods, in a direct attempt to establish a state religion that was fully responsive to the Nazis and that would not hinder them by the moral and ethical rules of Christianity. Such national spectacles aroused an enormous fervor in those people who participated and in the even greater crowds who watched—a fervor that communicated itself to the most important watcher of all, Chancellor Hitler, who not only knew very well how such emotions could be used to make people follow him but reached emotional exaltation himself as a result of this mass response to his will.

Some time before Hitler's rise to power, the International Olympic Committee had awarded the 1936 Olympic Games to the city of Berlin, capital of Germany. Upon Hitler's takeover of the German government, there seemed a good possibility that the Germans would refuse to hold the games; the Nazis had previously—before they were in power—fulminated against holding Olympic competitions in which "Nordic" Germans would compete with inferior "non-Aryans," an anti-Olympic organization had been formed in eighteen German universities, and the crudely anti-Semitic Nazi newspaper *Der Stürmer* had called the Olympics "an infamous festival dominated by Jews."

Hitler also realized that it would take a great deal of money to stage the Olympic Games. The world was still in the midst of a depression, and Germany was pouring as much money as it could into rearmament, in violation of its treaties—something that might become embarrassingly evident if foreign visitors overran the country. But Joseph Goebbels, Hitler's chief of propaganda, convinced his leader that the Olympics could be made into a global spectacle in which the Nazi tradition of showmanship would overwhelm the world with admiration for Nazi Germany. Toward the end of 1933 Hitler made the decision to go ahead with the Olympic Games.

The Germans sprang into action. They built an Olympic Village to house the male contestants, containing 150 one-story dormitories of brick or stone, housing sixteen, twenty, or twenty-four Olympians in double rooms with baths. (It was conveniently close to Staaken Airport, so that after the games it could be converted to military barracks.) In addition, there were a library, hospital, theater, recreation hall, and post office, all surrounded by carefully landscaped grounds. The relatively few women athletes were housed in less comfortable quarters near the sports field, in a single new building guarded by a high fence. There was a new stadium seating over 100,000 people, with a new and improved public address system, better than anything previously known. There were new electronic and photographic devices for scoring. Surrounding the stadium were a vast number of other sports fields occupying a total of 356 acres. Bus schedules were worked out in mathematical detail to carry all the athletes over the five miles between the village and the sports complex. Platoons of automobiles were made available for international Olympic officials. (Spectators during the games were to be amused and dismayed by one example of German thoroughness, however. During the three-hour noon break they were all required to leave the stadium so

The Olympic village, with one of the buses that carried the athletes to the stadium

DER JUGEND DER WELT
IA-202 630

that it could be cleaned—but outside, policemen politely but very firmly kept them from walking, let alone sitting or lying, on the newly sodded grass.)

In his quick rise to power, Hitler had shown many of the brutal characteristics for which he later became notorious. Torture, murder, and rigged trials were his common tools. Well known was his hatred for Jews, which dated back to the early years of his party when Nazi street gangs smashed shops owned by Jews and beat up Jewish people. After he became chancellor, the Nazis passed anti-Jewish laws and removed most Jews from government posts. In 1935 even stronger laws were enacted, depriving Jews of citizenship and civil rights and forbidding intermarriage between Jews and other Germans. Anti-Semitic posters appeared throughout Germany. The Nazis' attitude toward blacks was, if possible, even stronger than that toward Jews; they did not even consider the blacks human.

All of this led to discussion and debate in other nations as the time for the Berlin Olympics approached. The debate was most vigorous in the United States, and there it centered on one question: should the United States participate in the coming games or not? A basic thesis of all Olympic Games is that sportsmanship rises above any political or national considerations. One group felt that it was important in the face of Hitler's activities to uphold this principle by having Americans present at Berlin. An opposing group pointed out that Hitler himself was perverting the games for his own political advantage, and they felt that American participation could only help him. Much of the time, however, the argument seemed to lie between people who claimed there was nothing at all wrong with Nazi Germany (one U.S. Olympic official even announced that it did not concern him "one bit" about what was happening to Jews in Germany any more than it did about lynchings in the South) and those who were outraged because of Nazi policy toward Jews, toward blacks, toward labor unions, or toward the Christian churches. Finally the U.S. Amateur Athletic Union decided that United States participation would not imply endorsement of Nazi policies, and by the narrowest margin determined that an American team would join those of the other nations competing in Germany.

That American team was composed of 458 athletes, 76 of whom went to the Winter Olympics held in Bavaria several months before the summer games in Berlin. Most of the competitors going to the summer games sailed on the S.S. *Manhattan* on July 15. A single picket walked up and down the pier, carrying a sign reading: "Boycott Hitler Germany; fight for tolerance, freedom, and liberty."

The ship was not for the sole use of the athletes; it carried a number of commercial passengers as well. For them there was a bar, and soon it became evident that some of the athletes were also patronizing it. The officials in charge of the team issued a warning: beer was the only alcoholic beverage its members could drink, and they had to be in bed by midnight. When the ship docked at Hamburg the president of the American Olympic Committee, Avery Brundage, announced that Eleanor Holm Jarrett, the world's backstroke swimming champion, had been dropped from the team for violating these regulations.

In addition to having an athletic title, the beautiful Mrs. Jarrett was both a movie actress and a nightclub entertainer (for which activities Mr. Brundage had earlier tried to have her declared a professional), and so this announcement made large headlines. Perhaps the headlines were larger because her crime had been to drink champagne too often and too much with several of the newspapermen who were traveling aboard. Mrs.

Members of the American team waving from the deck of the S.S. Manhattan

Jarrett said that she was only one of several athletes who did the same thing. A petition asking for her reinstatement, signed by 220 of her teammates, did not sway Brundage from his decision. Snorted *Time* magazine: "A lurid and unnecessary scandal."

Aside from this one happening, not a great deal occurred during the voyage; the ship was like a floating gymnasium with athletes working out on several of the decks. The trip was slightly enlivened by an attack of appendicitis suffered by the 400-meter champion, Harold Smallwood. Otherwise, the high point came near the end of the voyage, when the athletes voted to determine the most beautiful woman among them (Joanna de Tuscan, the fencer), the handsomest man (Glenn Hardin, the 400-meter hurdle racer), the most popular woman (Katherine Rawls, the swimmer), and the most popular man (Glenn Cunningham, the runner). A close second for the most popular man was Jesse Owens.

Owens, a track star from Ohio State University, was one of ten blacks on the U.S. Team. They attracted some attention when the team reached Berlin—they were unusual sights in that city—but despite their curiosity, the Berliners were generally polite. And despite Nazi racial theories, the crowd in the big stadium was to show itself enthusiastic whenever the black Americans performed well.

The First Three Days

The sports in the Olympics ranged from shooting and horseback riding to swimming and track. Many events occurred at the same time. Only those drawing the largest audiences—particularly the track and field events—were held in the main stadium. The others took place in the sports complex surrounding it (where swimming had its own stadium for 20,000 spectators; and the enclosed hall for boxing, wrestling, and other indoor sports also accommodated 20,000) or in some cases—that of sailing, for example—completely outside the city of Berlin.

Track and field competition began in the big main stadium on Sunday, the day after the opening ceremonies. Adolf Hitler was present. One of the early events, the shot put, was won by Hans Woellke of Germany, who heaved the shot a distance of 53 feet, 1 13/16 inches—a new record. Also, this was the first time since the beginning of the modern Olympics in 1896 that Germany had had a champion in any of the track and field events. The audience went wild with enthusiasm, shouting Nazi "Heils." Woellke stood on the victor's stand to receive his gold medal and the potted miniature oak tree from the Black Forest that was presented to all winners. Hitler, greatly pleased by Woellke's feat, had the shot-putter brought up to his box to receive personal congratulations. (Woellke, a police sergeant, was soon afterward made a lieutenant.) So far as the Nazis were concerned, the games were off to a good start.

Then the Finns made a clean sweep of the 10,000-meter run, Ilmari Salminen in the lead, with other Finnish runners taking second and third place. Hitler was naturally less enthusiastic than he had been over the German accomplishment in the shot put, but he promptly invited the Finns to his box and gave them his personal congratulations.

Hilde (Tilly) Fleischer and Luise Krueger, both of them Germans, then took first and second places in the women's javelin throw, Miss Fleischer establishing a new Olympic record of 148 feet, 2 3/4 inches. The crowds cheered enthusiastically. The women were immediately taken up to Hitler's box for his congratulations.

Later, the United States carried off three first places in the men's high jump, and the winner and runner-up were both black! First place was taken by Cornelius Johnson of California, second by Dave Albritton of Ohio State. What would Chancellor Hitler, prophet of Nazi racial theories, do now? Hitler decided that it was late in the day and that rain threatened; he hurriedly got up and left the stadium, thereby avoiding any rain—as well as any need to shake the hand of the supposedly inferior black champion.

On Monday, August 3, Hitler was back. He saw Karl Hein of Germany set a new Olympic record by throwing the hammer 185 feet, 4 1/16 inches. Hein was quoted as saying that he did it because Hitler was watching: "I stood with my back to the field to start circling to throw. I looked up and saw the Führer watching my every move. Then I said to myself, 'Young fellow, show what you can do.' " During the competition, a group of boys of the Hitler Youth who occupied one section of the stadium began to chant, "Two for our Führer! Two for our Führer!" (meaning that they wanted Germany to win two medals for Hitler). Sure enough, second place in the hammer throw was also won by a German.

Once again the German spectators were vastly enthusiastic, shouting "Heil, heil," in unison until the stadium rang. But what of Hitler? He had learned his lesson; he could not congratulate some winners and fail to congratulate others without causing a reaction that might easily destroy the propaganda value of the whole Berlin Olympics. So he no longer congratulated any of the winners publicly—although he did meet the two German hammer-throwers under the stadium, out of public view, and express his pleasure at their success.

From Hitler's point of view, it was just as well that he followed this tactic, for the winner of the feature event of the afternoon, the 100-meter dash, was Jesse Owens, the American black. Owens took the lead at the start and held it all the way. Second was Ralph Metcalfe, another black. Hitler watched, but offered no congratulations to the victors.

Meanwhile, Owens, who was destined to be the outstanding star of the Berlin games, was working his way through the preliminaries of some of the other competitions. He was also competing in the broad jump (now called the long jump) and the 200-meter sprint. On Tuesday morning he readily qualified in the 200-meter event, breaking the Olympic record in the process.

In the broad-jump preliminaries he soon recognized that his major opponent was a German, Lutz Long, a tall, well-built, blond man who was the perfect example of a Nordic athlete—the Nazi ideal. Although Owens held the world record for the broad jump, he was now on unfamiliar ground; and

Above: *Hitler congratulating Tilly Fleischer, winner of the women's javelin throw.*
Below: *Cornelius Johnson took first place in the men's high jump*

USA

USA

when Long made his qualifying jump he broke the Olympic record. The two seemed to be well matched.

As Owens later recalled, while he was getting ready for his preliminary jump an American newsman came up to him and asked if it was true that Hitler had walked out on him, refusing to watch him jump. Owens looked over at the chancellor's box, and sure enough, it was empty. That this was, in fact, a calculated snub seems doubtful—after all, these were only preliminary trials and Hitler had watched while blacks, including Owens, competed in the main events. But the effect on Owens was to make him suddenly angry, so that he made a tremendous jump that outdistanced everyone else's—and one that was never counted because in his emotional turmoil he went half a foot beyond the takeoff point before he jumped, thereby committing a foul. (Owens disagreed entirely with the news reports that said he never jumped at all the first time.)

Attempting to keep himself under control on his next jump, Owens did not go far enough, and the try was no good. Now he had only one chance left to qualify, and he felt shaky. Hitler was still absent from that box. The vast German crowd seemed to be menacing; he felt they were hoping for him to fail. He had to clench his jaw to keep his teeth from chattering. His breathing came hard.

Suddenly he felt a hand on his arm and turned to look at the blond German, Lutz Long, who was viewing him with concern. Owens heard the man he considered his greatest enemy asking, "What has taken your goat?" The way Long used the

Above: *Dave Albritton, runner-up to Cornelius Johnson in the high jump*. Below: *Jesse Owens taking the 100-meter dash*

Jesse Owens with his
German friend and rival Lutz Long

American slang expression made Owens grin even as he shrugged off the question, but he involuntarily glanced toward Hitler's empty box.

Long realized the problem. "Is it what Chancellor Hitler did?" Then as Owens stumbled, not knowing what to say, Long told him what he must do to qualify in his one remaining opportunity: start to jump six inches behind the foul line and jump as hard as he could. In that way he need not be afraid of another foul and he would certainly cover enough distance.

And that is what Owens did. He measured his steps, put a towel beside the track six inches short of the takeoff board, and walked back to the starting point. He began his run, jumped as he came to the towel—and qualified. (Long and Owens became good friends as the result of this incident, and Owens continued to write to Long until the United States entered World War II. Lutz was killed in Africa in 1943.)

In the afternoon Owens won his quarter-final trial in the 200-meter series, duplicating the time of his earlier trial, 21.1, and thus breaking the record twice in a day. Then he returned to the broad-jump pit. There, in the final competition, his first jump was longer than any of the others, until Lutz Long equaled it, to the enormous pleasure of the audience. On the next jump, Owens reached a distance of slightly over 26 feet—the longest such jump in Olympic history, several inches beyond Long's distance. Owens's last jump took him 26 feet, 5 21/64 inches, an even greater record. Long's best jump of 25 feet, 9 27/32 inches was itself a great accomplishment, surpassing the last Olympic record and exceeding anything done by a German athlete in any of the past Olympics, but it was far short of Owens's leap. Even so, Hitler received Long and warmly congratulated him—under the stands, out of sight. As the *New York Times* report put it, Hitler waited "until his emissaries had pried Long loose from Owens, with whom he was affectionately walking along the track arm and arm." The German dictator did not congratulate Owens, the winner.

There were two major women's events that day, the discus throw and the 100-meter dash. The first was won by Gisela Mauermayer of Germany, the blond, six-foot-tall world champion, whose neat but robust appearance led writers to use such terms as "virginal beauty" and "a magnificent woman." She set a new Olympic record. (In addition to her physical prowess, Miss Mauermayer also had a brain; she was later to earn *two* doctor's degrees.)

The 100-meter dash was won by Helen Stephens, an already famous eighteen-year-old from Missouri, who also set a new world record—11.5 seconds, better than many male athletes could do, and a record that would not be broken until 1960. Miss Stephens was a favorite with the crowd, and was probably the best-known female athlete competing in these games (her only rival in this regard was Eleanor Holm Jarrett, who was not allowed to compete). She was followed in order by a Polish and a German girl. At a time when women athletes were gaining more and more recognition (women's track and field events had first been included in the Olympics only as recently as 1928), Helen Stephens was the much admired heroine of the day.

Later, Hitler met both Mauermayer and Stephens privately and offered his congratulations on their achievements. Miss Stephens was the only American so honored during the Olympics.

Above: *Gisela Mauermayer, winner of the women's discus throw.*
Below: *Helen Stephens, eighteen-year-old winner of the 100-meter dash, a record not broken until 1960*

Earlier that same Tuesday Glenn Hardin of Mississippi had easily won the 400-meter hurdles, although he set no records in doing so. The Nazis could perhaps take some comfort in the fact that, although the event had been won by an American, he was at least a white American. But then came Owens's triumph and finally, toward the end of the day, the astonishing 800-meter finals.

John Woodruff, a black freshman at the University of Pittsburgh, a tall, slim young man, was one of the U.S. 800-meter competitors. He did not have much athletic experience, and at the start he found himself boxed in, surrounded by the bodies of all the other competitors. He dropped back to a jog and let the others all get ahead. Then he moved to the outside, really started running–and passed them all. He slowed for a breather and Phil Edwards, a Canadian black, took the opportunity to sprint ahead of Woodruff; and then the Italian competitor, Mario Lanzi, began to come up behind him. Woodruff found an extra reserve of energy, swung out around Edwards and passed him, and, going into the home stretch, was four yards in the lead. Lanzi continued to move up, however, closing the distance. Woodruff hit the tape two yards ahead of the Italian. Edwards was third. (Because of the unorthodox zigzag pattern of his running, Woodruff ran some fifty meters farther than anyone else.)

Black Americans had won nearly every major event of the day. The Nazi newspaper *Der Angriff* (*The Attack*), found a unique way of salving the feelings of Hitler and any others who shared his racial views. The black athletes, it declared, were neither American nor human, but merely "black auxiliaries" of

John Woodruff,
winner of the 800-meter competition

the U.S. team. “Actually, the Yankees, heretofore invincible, have been the great disappointment of the games,” the paper said. The only fair way to keep score was to consider the first Germans who followed the blacks as the true winners! The Nazi paper solemnly presented a scoring system based on this thesis.

Most of the German spectators, however, had no thought of such foolishness. The appearance of Jesse Owens on the field now caused them to cry “Yessa Ovens” (their way of pronouncing his name); and Owens was followed in the streets of Berlin and into the Olympic Village by people who wanted his autograph or simply wanted to take pictures of him.

Outside the Stadium

Outside the playing fields, Berlin was in holiday dress. The five miles of what was known as the Olympic Highway, through the city and out to the stadium, was lined with long banners that hung nearly to the ground from fifty-foot flagpoles. Blue banners carrying the symbolic Olympic rings alternated with red ones displaying the Nazi swastika. Other rows of similar poles along the edges of the sidewalks also flew banners; and in addition, each of these inner poles supported a circular oil painting of a different German city, wreathed in evergreens. At street intersections, taller poles flying bigger flags were wound with ropes of evergreen and gold. Loudspeakers were spaced along the entire way at intervals of an eighth of a mile. During the events, the games were described over these speakers to the crowds that gathered to listen; afterward, in the evenings, waltzes and quickstep marches were played.

The Nazis also held other meetings and ceremonies. There was a reception in the Berlin City Hall for the winners of past Olympics. A congress on physical education brought students to Berlin from all over the world and lasted for a month. An International Sporting Press Congress gave all of the sportswriters who were assembled for the Olympics something to do in their spare time. In the nearby countryside, there were rallies for automobiles, motorcycles, and canoes. The canoe—actually the folding boat of the Germans, built much like a kayak—was vastly popular, and thousands of people flocked to participate in that rally.

In addition to ceremonies linked directly to the Olympics or to physical sports, there were artistic and musical events, military parades, and parties. There was even a lecture on "The History of the Horse in Asia"; the reason for this presentation, the Germans explained without a flicker of humor, was that the ancient Greeks held discussions of philosophy during their Olympic Games.

Normally in Berlin a military guard was posted only at the War Ministry, where there was a daily guard-mount ceremony during which the guard was changed. The precision-drilled German troops going through their ceremony were a popular attraction both for Berliners and for tourists. On special occasions sentries were also posted at the headquarters of the Berlin command, and a guard-changing ceremony was held there; the Olympics certainly were a special occasion, and so the Berlin command held its ceremony during the games. Hermann Göring, head of the German air force, was never to be outdone, and he saw to it that during this time a guard of gray-uniformed airmen was posted at his headquarters and that a daily military ceremony was also held there when the guard was changed. As a result, visitors and Germans could watch three different guard-changing ceremonies, and the troops marching to and from them seemed to be always in the streets. Foreigners were startled to see, marching solemnly along beside the soldiers, not only the small boys of Berlin but also plump, middle-aged Berliners.

One of the major social gatherings at the time was a party given by Joseph Goebbels, the Nazi propaganda minister, a short, dark man, who presided in a white double-breasted suit, and Mrs. Goebbels, who wore white organdy. The party was for the International Olympic Committee and other visitors of im-

Berlin in holiday dress
for the Olympics

PELZHAUS
PELZWAREN-HAUS
J. Seifer
Pelzwaren

portance. The highest level of diplomatic society attended, as well as opera singers, writers, dancers, and other artists. There were over a thousand guests. The party was held on an island in the Havel River near the Berlin suburb of Potsdam, in a park that had been the private recreation spot of Frederick the Great. Lights were strung through the trees, girl pages held burning torches, there were fireworks and dance bands. One writer compared it to a scene from *The Arabian Nights*. It was generally acknowledged to be a wonderful party. Other high-ranking Nazis gave big parties as well, but none was as splendid as that of the propaganda chief.

Less exalted Berliners also felt the surge of Olympic enthusiasm. They watched Chancellor Hitler's long, open Mercedes cruising through the avenues, with the dictator standing bolt upright in the front seat and four cars of steel-helmeted guards following, running close to the curbs on either side of the street. They saw the parades and processions. They listened to the loudspeakers. They observed the airplanes and dirigibles overhead. They heard or read of important foreigners–Charles Lindbergh, the American flier, for example–who were in the city, and perhaps they saw a few of them. They rubbed elbows on the streets with athletes and tourists from countries all over the world. As one result, the Olympic stadium was jammed for important events and many more people wanted tickets than could get them. Even such an exotic attraction–for the Germans–as an exhibition baseball game drew crowds larger than any at a World Series game in the United States, even though most of the people had little idea of what was going on out on the field. (A German sports expert later gave an explanation to his countrymen, beginning: "Both teams appeared with nine players; the team with red stockings attacked first.") To help as many people see the Olympic events as possible, the Germans made use of television in a major way for the first time in history; the big cameras watching the events in the stadium were connected by cable to halls where people could watch the pictures. The technical problems would not be solved for years to come, however, and the viewers were disappointed when they saw only vaguely moving shadows.

The Next Four Days

On Wednesday, August 5, the main stadium was again packed. There were showers and the weather was cold, but these things did not deter the audience. The morning hours on Wednesday were taken up by the preliminary trials for various events and by the beginning of the 50,000-meter walk. The competitors started off out of the stadium on their long walk, which took them around the nearby countryside and back to finish at the stadium again in the late afternoon. The winners began to arrive in the stadium just as the most important event of the day, the final running of the 200-meter dash, was about to start. The first 50,000-meter walker was Harold Whitlock of Great Britain, who set a new world record of 4 hours, 30 minutes, 41.4 seconds. But the crowd, anxiously waiting the start of the 200-meter dash, paid little attention to this feat, or to the fact that Ken Carpenter of California spun the discus to a new Olympic record of 165 feet, 7 29/64 inches.

There were six competitors in the 200-meter finals, one from Canada, two from the Netherlands, one from Switzerland, and two from the United States. Chancellor Hitler sat watching in his box as the rain fell in a steady drizzle and the evening gloom began to close in. The track was soaked by water, and the wind gusted fitfully. At the gun, Jesse Owens was first away; he remained in front and won easily, setting a new Olympic record of 20.7 seconds—despite the fact that the course lay

Ken Carpenter throws the discus to a new Olympic record

around a curve and that he had to buck a quartering wind. The crowd rose to cheer as Owens thus carried off his third gold medal of the Olympics. Second was Matthew Robinson of Pasadena College, and he was also black. As the stadium echoed to the crowd's enthusiastic chants of "O-vens, O-vens," in honor of Jesse's third Olympic win, the rain began to fall more heavily. Chancellor Hitler rose and departed, without stopping to see Owens step to the victor's block and receive his medal and potted oak tree. The rain was a good excuse; but as some of the news reports pointed out, it looked very much as though Hitler had retreated in confusion from his own grand stadium in the face of this third triumph by the black Jesse Owens.

The competition for the pole vault had been going on during a large part of the day. Now in the rain and growing darkness, and with the ground steadily becoming more muddy, the event was won by Earle Meadows of Southern California, with a new Olympic record of 14 feet, 3 1/4 inches. The contest had taken five hours to complete—longer even than the walking race—and when it was over, eleven men still were tied for sixth place. The competitors were all bone-weary from their efforts. Shuhei Nishida, of Japan, was second, and Sueo Oye, also of Japan, was third.

On Thursday the weather was cool and dry, good for athletic competition. That day Gerhard Stöck of Germany won the javelin throw. He was a surprise winner—Finland and Sweden had previously held the honors in the event—and the German crowd was ecstatic as they shouted out "Heils." Naoto Tajima of Japan won the running hop, skip, and jump. Forrest Towns, an American from Georgia, was off to a slow start in the 110-meter hurdles race, but at the fourth hurdle he drew ahead to win by eight feet; Donald Finlay of Britain was second, and Fritz Pollard, a black American from the University of North Dakota, was third.

In the women's 80-meter hurdles, the first four racers were so close that they were all clocked at 11.7 seconds. The new photographic equipment, however, saved the day. While the contestants stood waiting and the audience sat tensely, technicians developed the motion-picture film and judges announced that Trebisonda Valla of Italy was first, Anny Steuer of Germany second, and Elizabeth Taylor of Canada third. By that time Miss Taylor, tired of waiting, had wandered away and could not be found for the presentation of the medals.

The event of the day was the men's 1,500-meter run. Twelve finalists took part. At the start, Jerry Cornes of Great Britain took the lead. Then Glenn Cunningham, the Kansas athlete who held the world's record for the mile, moved into the lead. A Swede, Eric Ny, passed Cunningham in the third lap; but then he was passed by Cunningham, who again took the lead.

As the leading runners entered the final backstretch, Jack Lovelock of New Zealand—a slim, 135-pound redhead who had been a Rhodes scholar and was studying medicine in London—began his final sprint, past Ny, past Cunningham, moving quickly ahead of all the others. Cunningham and Luigi Beccali, the Italian who held the previous Olympic championship and who was now coming up fast, were hot on his heels. The two pursuing champions called on their full reserves of energy, but they still were unable to catch Lovelock, who, standing out in his neat black costume, sailed along with apparent ease, well ahead.

Lovelock crossed the line first with a time of 3 minutes, 47.8 seconds, a new world record. So fast had the competition been that all four of the men who followed him broke the previous Olympic record. Now there were three popular heroes of these Olympics: Jesse Owens, for winning so many events so consistently; Helen Stephens, as the outstanding female athlete; and Jack Lovelock, for winning a single event so brilliantly.

Friday morning's developments consisted largely of activities making up the decathlon, the ten-part competition intended to determine the best all-around athlete. (The parts consist of the 100-meter dash, running broad (long) jump, 16-pound shot put, high jump, 400-meter run, 110-meter hurdles, discus, pole vault, javelin throw, and 1,500-meter run; each contestant must compete in all of the events, which are staged separately from the similar events in which specialized champions are chosen.) In the afternoon the semifinals were held for the regular (nondecathlon) 400-meter event, but the American star, Harold Smallwood, was not there. He was the athlete who had had an attack of appendicitis on the ship on his way to Europe; now the appendicitis had returned so violently that Smallwood—at almost the same moment as the trials began—was undergoing an operation in a Berlin hospital.

The 5,000-meter finals, with fifteen participants, comprised the first major contest on Friday. The three Finnish runners soon moved well into the lead, but toward the end of the race one of them, Ilmari Salminen, somehow collided with

Above: *Gerhard Stöck, surprise winner of the men's javelin throw, saluting Hitler.*
Below: *Two of the popular heroes of the Olympics: Helen Stephens and Jesse Owens*

SUOMI
USA

the other two, fell, and was left behind. The winner was Gunnar Höckert, and the runner-up Lauri Lehtinen, both of them Finns. Höckert set a new Olympic record of 14 minutes, 22.2 seconds. Third was John Henry Jonsson of Sweden.

Then came the 400-meter finals. Arthur Brown of Great Britain, a student at Cambridge, took the early lead; but Archie Williams, the black athlete from the University of California, and James Lu Valle, another black from UCLA, both passed him in the backstretch. Entering the homestretch, Brown again passed Lu Valle and moved up on Williams; but the latter stayed ahead to win the race. At the end Williams, Brown, Lu Valle, and Roberts, another British runner, were so close that reporters commented a blanket could have covered all four of them. Once again the black Americans had won their medals.

On Saturday, in the 3,000-meter steeplechase, Volmari Iso-Hollo of Finland came in first, setting a new Olympic record with the time of 9 minutes, 3.8 seconds; he thus maintained his position as Olympic champion in this event, which he had won at the previous Olympics, held in Los Angeles in 1932.

A major event of this day was the 1,500-meter run that completed the decathlon. It was scheduled in the big stadium for the late afternoon. But the Olympic authorities inserted in the program immediately before it an hour-long gymnastic exhibition by 1,200 Swedes, and serious sports fans squirmed and fumed while the gymnasts went through their graceful maneuvers. As a result of the delay, the decathlon was completed under floodlights ten and a half hours after the morning session had begun.

Archie Williams in the 400-meter finals

801
865

Just before the start of the 1,500-meter decathlon run, the announcer stated over the public address system that Glenn Morris, the American who was the leading contender, would have to better a time of 4 minutes, 32 seconds in this event in order for his total decathlon score to set a new record. Morris had never run that fast in his life. The tall, slim athlete had already been through the wringing competition of the other decathlon events, and he was obviously tired. But he threw himself into the 1,500-meter race with clumsy intensity, keeping in front of the other runners until the last lap, when a Belgian pulled ahead of him. Then in the final straightaway Morris surged ahead again, crossing the finish line first. His total time was the best he had ever done, 4 minutes, 33.3 seconds–but it was over a second too slow to set a new record! The sympathetic audience groaned. Then the announcer came on the public address system to say that there had been an error in the previous computation and it had not been necessary for Morris to do better than 4:32 after all; he was the decathlon winner with a total of 7,900 points and had indeed set a new record. Robert Clark and Jack Parker, both from the United States, were second and third.

Glenn Morris, number 801, winner of the decathlon

The Eighth Day

The eighth day of the Berlin Olympics and the final day of the track and field events saw a development in the American team that led to violent argument at the time and that still causes knowledgeable people to take opposite sides when the matter is discussed.

The 400-meter relay was run that day. The United States team consisted of Foy Draper, Frank Wykoff, Sam Stoller, and Marty Glickman. Before the event was run, officials of the U.S. team dropped Stoller and Glickman from the team and substituted Jesse Owens and Ralph Metcalfe for them. Stoller and Glickman, who were Jewish, became the only American athletes who made the trip to Berlin but never participated in any of the events there. And the fact that they were Jews led to accusations that they were taken from the team because of Nazi influence.

The participants later told what they thought of the substitution. Glickman felt that several influences were at work. The American coaches were afraid of the German relay team and wanted to strengthen their own by using Owens and Metcalfe in place of two of the regular members. One of the Olympic coaches was from the University of Southern California, as were Wykoff and Draper, and Glickman thought that the coach naturally wanted his own athletes to run; therefore Stoller and Glickman were the ones replaced. But Glickman also knew that several key officials of the U.S. team were members of the pro-Nazi America First Committee, and he did not discount the fact that these men had not wanted Jewish athletes to participate. Stoller, on the other hand, was inclined to think the change was made as it was solely to keep the Southern California athletes on the team when the champion performers, Owens and Metcalfe, were added.

In any event, the evening before the race there was a discussion about the matter that ended in bitter words among players and coaches that have echoed ever since. And whatever the motives were behind the decision, the incident raised one question that has been asked more and more often about the modern Olympic Games. Do they, as advertised, promote sportsmanship and individual competition? Or does the drive to win often take precedence over all human values?

As it happened, the U.S. team won handsomely with a new world record of 39.8 seconds, and the performance of the two black Americans, Owens and Metcalfe, could scarcely have cheered the Nazi racial theorists any more than if Jewish athletes had competed. Also, Owens was able to win his fourth gold medal. But the situation surrounding this 400-meter relay race seemed even stranger late that day when it became evident that the American officials had left their 1,600-meter relay team intact and had not substituted the other two black superstars, Archie Williams and Jimmy Lu Valle, for men on that team. The British won the 1,600-meter relay.

The most prestigious event on this last day of the track and field championships was the most famous of all, the marathon. The runners started out of the stadium in midafternoon, following a more-than-26-mile course through the surrounding countryside. The defending champion, Juan Carlos Zabala of Argentina, held the lead. Kitei Son, a Korean student running for Japan (which then governed Korea), and Ernest Harper, an Englishman, were next. Harper kept advising the young Korean to hold back—not to try to pass Zabala but to let him burn himself out. Sure enough, two thirds of the way through, Zabala slowed down, moved off the track, and abandoned the race.

Meanwhile, in the stadium the women's 400-meter relay race was taking place. The two major contending teams were those of Germany and the United States. As Hitler watched, the German girls made a splendid start, and at the last exchange Marie Dollinger of Germany led Betty Robinson of the United States by eight yards. The German spectators cheered wildly. Miss Dollinger ran up to her teammate Ilse Dörffeldt to pass the baton—and, instead, it dropped to the track. A horrified silence fell over the crowd as the American Helen Stephens swept easily on to victory and the German team proceeded to have hysterics. Hitler rose to the occasion, calling the four German girls up to his box and trying to console them by saying that it had only been an accident and they were certainly the best team competing.

Another women's event held this same day was the high jump. It resulted in a three-way tie at 5 feet, 3 inches. After the jump-off was held, Ibolya Csák of Hungary was first, Dorothy Odam of Britain was second, and Elfriede Kaun of Germany was third. The German favorite, Dora Ratjen, placed only fourth. During the course of the Olympics several Germans had muttered darkly that some of the female champions should be examined to find out if they were not really men, and at least one German newspaper expressed concern about the possibility of men competing as women. Ironically, the only known case in these Olympics of a man pretending to be a woman (which came to light only after World War II), was the German Dora Ratjen—whose real name was Hermann, and who claimed to have been forced into the masquerade by Hitler Youth leaders. Perhaps even more ironic is the fact that he did not even attain one of the first three places.

In the late afternoon the packed spectators were alerted by a fanfare of trumpets and stood up almost in unison to look at the tunnellike stadium gate through which the marathon runners would appear. In a moment the first of them burst out of the dark tunnel into the sunshine; it was Kitei Son. Running

American track and field stars:
from left, Jesse Owens, Ralph Metcalfe,
Foy Draper, and Frank Wykoff

265
382

strongly and looking straight ahead, apparently not even aware of the surging cheers of the crowd, he came on into the stadium and neatly broke the tape, establishing a new Olympic record of 2 hours, 29 minutes, 19.2 seconds. He jogged on down the track a short distance, sat down in the grass beside it, and took off his shoes. Then he got up and ran off to his dressing room before the next runner, Ernest Harper, even came in sight. Harper crossed the finish line, staggered off the track, and collapsed in the grass; helping hands quickly laid blankets over him. He was still there when the third man, Shoryu Nan, another Korean student competing for Japan, ran through the gate. (Kitei Son later told newsmen that he owed his victory to Harper's advice.)

Kitei Son passing
Ernest Harper in the marathon

Outside Berlin

The Olympic Games and the other celebrations in Berlin were held against an increasingly grim world backdrop. Grimmest of the international events was the Spanish Civil War. In Spain a leftist government held the reins of legal power while a rightist group, under General Francisco Franco, rebelled against it. As *The New York Times* summed it up: "Should the revolt triumph—and, viewed from Madrid, it cannot win without foreign intervention—a Fascist regime would be the result, against which rebellion would continue until drowned in blood. Should the sedition be suppressed—and that certainly will be a long business—the liberal republic of 1931 must perish in the process. Two extremes are at each other's throats. . . ."

Headlines about the Olympics in most American papers were next to bigger headlines reporting that four rebel or Nationalist columns of troops were converging on Madrid. General Emilio Mola, who commanded those columns, remarked in October that he had an equally effective fifth column within the city—an organized subversive group. The term *fifth column* soon became an accepted one for such a group.

Each side slaughtered with such fierce abandon prisoners of war and civilians who disagreed with it that newspapers were soon filled with horror-stricken accounts of what the Spaniards were doing to each other. While the Olympics progressed, German and Italian aircraft arrived in Spain to bolster the rebels,

Above: *Hitler and Göring enjoying the games.* Below: *A street in Madrid during the Spanish Civil War*

and the mayor of one French town on the Spanish border reported that two hundred volunteers had passed through to fight for the Loyalists: "only high-grade men, like aviators, machine-gunners, motorcyclists, etc., have been accepted, and, moreover, only those who are members in good standing of the French Socialist party. . . ." Meanwhile, Russia promised supplies and money to the Loyalists and began to ship them arms, while at the same time holding a practice air-raid alert in Leningrad.

Smaller headlines were no more cheerful. Italy had recently attacked and conquered Ethiopia, although skirmishes between Italian troops and Ethiopian bands continued there in the more isolated areas. Russia was accusing Japan of plotting to attack it, and the Japanese continued to threaten parts of China. Britain was starting down the path of appeasement that led to the sell-out of Czechoslovakia at Munich. Germany had been busily fortifying the island of Helgoland in the North Sea, in violation of the Treaty of Versailles, and during the first week of the Olympics the question was raised in Parliament as to what the British government intended to do about it. Anthony Eden, then Foreign Secretary, said it would do nothing at all for fear of upsetting negotiations that were going forward with Germany. At the same time the British government "terminated assurances" to Turkey and Yugoslavia that Britain would protect them against Italy. Mussolini, said Mr. Eden, had assured those countries of his friendship.

The Belgians were thinking aloud that they might abandon their alliance with France and revert to the neutral position they had held, with so little success, before the First World War. President Eduard Beneš of Czechoslovakia said that that country was willing to grant "the utmost concessions" to its minorities—meaning the Germans who lived there—but that it must reject any "external attempt to interfere with the republic's domestic affairs." In other words, he was telling Hitler to keep hands off—but as it turned out, no one was listening.

Other Events

Of the dozens of sports outside the track and field category, a few are of special interest.

Foremost among them are swimming and diving. Most of the crowded spectators for these sports (there were usually some 30,000 people crammed into stands intended for 20,000) were German, and they were much, and sometimes loudly, disappointed as event came after event and the German contestants made a very poor showing.

In men's swimming the Americans and Japanese divided most of the honors, although Ferenc Csik (pronounced "Sheik") of Hungary won the 100-meter freestyle; two Japanese were second and third. The 400-meter freestyle was won by Jack Medica of Seattle, who came from behind in a final dash during the last 40 meters to edge out the noted Shumpei Uto of Japan; another Japanese was third. Eighteen-year-old Adolph Kiefer of Chicago, the world champion, as expected won the 100-meter backstroke, taking the lead by the 10-meter mark and holding it all the way, with another American and a Japanese finishing in second and third place. Tetsuo Hamuro of Japan won the 200-meter breaststroke, while a German placed second and another Japanese third. The Japanese team finished the 800-meter relay 11.5 seconds before the American team; the Hungarians followed 9.2 seconds after the Americans.

During these events the spectators were puzzled and sometimes confused because the Americans seemed to be wearing the symbol of their most vigorous opponents, the Japanese. At that time men's tank suits still modestly had tops, and on those worn by swimmers from the United States there appeared the rising sun of Japan. The stars and stripes of the United States were also on the suits, but this symbol had faded and was not as evident as the Japanese emblem. The suits were left over from a long-past meet between Japan and the United States; the American team did not have a great deal of money in those depression days and had to make do with whatever they could get.

The men's diving events were almost a clean sweep by the Americans. The springboard diving was won by Richard Degener of Detroit, followed by Marshall Wayne and Al Greene. The high diving was won by Wayne, a Miamian, with Elbert Root second. The only non-American to win a place in the diving events was Hermann Stork, a German, and he took third place. The handsome, blond Wayne had the poise of an actor and the ability to win the sympathy of his audience. He was a clear favorite of the largely German crowd, even though the repeated failures of their own contestants left them not in the best of moods.

While the men's swimming events were largely an American and Japanese show, the results of the women's events turned out to be much more international. In the 100-meter freestyle, eighteen-year-old Hendrika Mastenbroek of Holland started fifth, was in third place by the 80-meter mark, then with a sudden drive broke into second place at 90 meters, ending with the same official time as Jeannette Campbell of Argentina, but in fact a split instant ahead of her; Gisela Arndt of Germany was third. The Dutch girl also won the 400-meter freestyle, with a Dane second and an American third. The 200-meter breaststroke was won by Hideko Maehata of Japan, while a German and a Dane were second and third (the Danish girl, Inge Sorensen, was twelve years old). The 100-meter backstroke was enlivened by the presence in the stands of the glamorous champion Eleanor Holm Jarrett, who had been barred from competition by Avery Brundage; the tiny Mrs. Jarrett stood on

Winner of the springboard diving Marjorie Gestring (left), and second-place runner-up Katherine Rawls

her seat so that she could see better, screaming encouragement for the American Edith Mottridge, who even so only came in third—the Dutch Dina Senff was first and the talented Hendrika Mastenbroek was second in this event. (The achievements of Miss Mastenbroek seem even more outstanding, considering that it was later discovered she had an obscure blood disease that prevented her body from receiving the normal amount of oxygen.)

The women's diving events were just as much an American success as were the men's events. In the high-platform diving the blond Mrs. Dorothy Poynton Hill, whose attractive appearance rivaled that of Mrs. Jarrett (one reporter called Mrs. Hill "the most pulchritudinous of all the female competitors in these increasingly feminine Olympics"), easily won first place; Velma Dunn of the United States was second and Käthe Köhler of Germany was third. The springboard diving was won by Marjorie Gestring, a petite blond thirteen-year-old who, like Mrs. Hill, came from Los Angeles, and who attracted some attention by lugging around with her as a mascot (when she was out of the water) an extra-large stuffed cat. Katherine Rawls of the United States was second in the event, and Mrs. Hill was third.

Basketball appeared on the Olympic schedule largely through the efforts of the Americans, but the rules for Olympic competition had been drawn up by European officials, with results that sometimes baffled players from the country where the game began. One rule barred any players taller than 6 feet 3 inches; but the Americans protested this rule so strongly (it would have disqualified several of their key players) that it was waived for this Olympics. When Dr. James A. Naismith, the American originator of basketball, arrived in Berlin, he was firmly snubbed by the Olympic officials and could only get in to see the games when some of the players gave him tickets.

The games were played outdoors, on old clay tennis courts, and at times in windy and rainy weather. For some of the later games the American team wore makeshift uniforms because their lockers were rifled in the middle of the series and their uniforms stolen. The final result was a North American sweep: the United States placed first, Canada second, and Mexico third.

One of the lesser-known but more grueling events was the pentathlon, a contest in which most of the competitors and all of the winners in 1936 were army officers. It supposedly represented the rigors that would be encountered by a military messenger traveling through enemy territory, and while its events may seem to have been contrived by a writer of adventure fiction, there is no question that they gave the contestants about as difficult a workout as a human being could withstand. First there was a 5,000-meter cross-country horse race; the hypothetical messenger would have to avoid roads, so the course went directly through forests and across swamps, rivers, and ravines. Next the messenger was supposed to encounter an enemy swordsman and to fight his way past; in this case, however, as there were forty-one contestants, each one had to fight forty duels; the fencing, done with the épée, began at 10:00 A.M. and continued until 10:30 P.M. After that the messenger supposedly met a sniper and had to finish him off; each contestant fired twenty shots with a pistol at a target shaped like a man. Then came a 300-meter swimming race and finally a 4,000-meter cross-country foot race. The winner of the pentathlon was Oberleutnant Gotthardt Handrick of Germany, a fighter pilot, who was immediately promoted to captain by Hitler. Handrick had not been first in any of the events of the pentathlon, but he had an excellent score in most of them and the best average. Second was Lieutenant Charles Leonard of the United States, who was also the best pistol shot. Third was Captain Silvano Abba of Italy, also the best horseman.

In the men's fencing competition the Italians won the team events for épée and foils, and the Hungarians the team event for the saber. Giulio Gaudini and Franco Riccardi, both Italian, won the individual foils and épée competitions respectively; Endre Kabos, a Hungarian, won the individual saber competition. But it was in women's fencing that the real drama emerged.

Women's fencing consisted only of individual foils competition. As the elimination matches progressed, it became evident that three of the contestants were of the highest quality. Best known of these was Helene Mayer of Germany, who, despite her blond, Nordic appearance (she was a big girl and wore her yellow hair braided and wrapped around her head) had a Jewish father. She had won first place for Germany in the 1928 Olympics and since then had been world champion at two different times. After competing in the 1932 Olympics, which were held at Los Angeles and in which she did not do well, she decided to remain in the United States and attend the University of Southern California. As the Nazis stepped up their anti-Semitic campaign, the sporting world was startled in 1933 to learn that Miss Mayer's home organization, the Offenbach Fencing Club, had expelled her because of her Jewish father.

At about that time, Dr. Theodor Lewald was removed as president of the German Olympic Committee because he had a Jewish ancestor. The International Olympic Committee became alarmed, and a movement developed within it to take the 1936 Olympic Games away from Germany unless German Jewish athletes were allowed to participate. The Nazis, by this time eager to have the games, promised faithfully that German Jews could participate—and at the same time rigged the selection process within Germany so that no Jews were able to compete. Miss Mayer, however, was famous and was living in the United States, where a press largely unsympathetic to the Nazis was watching carefully to see what happened. As a result, she became a member of the German team. (Similarly, Rudi Ball, a German Jew who had been living in France, was invited to join the German ice hockey team, and he accepted.) Miss Mayer publicly said that she was pleased to represent Germany, and the German Olympic officials helpfully declared that she was "Aryan"—thus from their own peculiar point of view making her presence legitimate.

The other two major contestants in the women's foils at Berlin were Ilona Schacherer-Elek, a slim, dark Hungarian Jew who had been European champion for the past two years, and Ellen Preis, a firm-jawed young Austrian who had won the gold medal at the 1932 Olympics. As the final competition developed into a three-way struggle between these young women, with all of the political and racial overtones involved, spectators began to pack the fencing grounds.

In the contest between Schacherer-Elek and Mayer, two opponents who otherwise were closely matched, the Hungarian girl soon realized that she could make the German one nervous

Contestants in the Pentathlon, one of the more grueling Olympic events

by posing and behaving in an exaggerated manner. This tactic brought the Hungarian victory in two out of three of their encounters (with results of 3–2, 4–4, and 5–4). Mayer, however, then moved ahead in matches with others, so that she and Schacherer-Elek were tied in points.

In the final, tense match, before a packed audience, Mayer met the Austrian Ellen Preis. Their first score was 2–2. The players and spectators became even more tense. Their next score was 3–3. The tension grew. Their third and final score was 4–4. Fantastically, it was a draw. But there were no more matches; the judges awarded the positions on points. Ilona Schacherer-Elek was first, Helene Mayer second, and Ellen Preis third.

As they later stood on the platform in the big stadium to receive their medals, Helene Mayer snapped a perfect Nazi salute toward Hitler, and the crowd roared.

The Ending

The last day of the Berlin Olympics, August 16, fell on a Sunday. The athletic events of the day were largely concerned with horsemanship, a sport about which most of the big crowd knew very little—but a sport that was gentlemanly and attractive to watch.

As sunset approached, the Nazi showmanship of the closing ceremonies came into play. The sun sank behind the five symbolic Olympic rings suspended between two towers at the western end of the stadium. Then at the exact moment of sunset a single cannon was heard. The deep bell in the tower outside the stadium began to toll. Somewhere out of sight, trumpeters sounded a fanfare; at the same instant, searchlights around the outside of the stadium shot their powerful beams upward. Then the beams tilted slowly inward until they met in the sky above, forming a vast tent of light over all.

As the fanfare ended, the flag bearers of the national teams marched in single file onto the field in the opposite order to that in which they had entered during the opening ceremonies; Germany was now first, the United States second, and so on. The flags formed in a floodlit line before a podium to which mounted the president of the International Olympic Committee, the Belgian Count Henri Baillet-Latour. In a brief, graceful speech Baillet-Latour thanked the German people and Hitler for their hospitality and ended by announcing that the next—the eleventh—Olympic Games, four years hence, were to be in Tokyo. (Because of World War II those Tokyo Olympics were never held; the next Olympic Games were not until 1948, and they were in London.)

At the end of this speech, the Berlin Philharmonic Or-

chestra (with extra musicians added for the occasion) and chorus began to render the Beethoven hymn "The Flame Dies." A distant—but not too distant—artillery salute, fired at carefully spaced intervals, provided solemn background. Then out of the darkness, into the floodlighting that illuminated the flag bearers, came tall, white-clad girls walking in columns of twos, each carrying a small laurel wreath. Each girl stopped before one of the flag bearers; the colors were lowered; and a girl fastened a laurel wreath to the top of each flagstaff.

The orchestra and chorus changed to another song, the white-clad girls marched off the field, and spotlights suddenly illuminated the six sailors who were lowering the Olympic flag from the main pole; the flag was gathered in by members of the German Olympic team, who were dressed all in white. The musicians became silent and the Olympic flame, which had burned steadily throughout the games, was now permitted to lower and burn out as some unseen hand turned off its fuel.

The members of the German team carried the flag to the field in front of Hitler's box and attached it to a short staff. An honor guard of German fencers with weapons in hand escorted it to the podium in midfield, where now stood the Bürgermeister of Berlin. He accepted the flag and promised to keep it for four years until it would be used again in Tokyo. The public address system then proclaimed: "I call the youth of the world to Tokyo!"

The orchestra began a specially composed farewell piece, "The Games Are Ended." The great mass of people stood, then began to sway with the music, many crossing arms to hold

The Olympic flame at Berlin

hands with those on either side. The orchestra played its last notes; the final official ceremonies were over.

But there remained one unofficial, spontaneous ceremony. Quickly the sound grew and spread through the stadium, ringing louder and louder as the audience saluted Hitler: *"Sieg Heil! Sieg Heil! Sieg Heil!"*

The Results

Because in theory the contests of the Olympic Games are between athletes or teams and not between nations, no official scores are announced. As one consequence, people who are interested in national totals must use their own methods of computing them—a practice that may lead to honest differences in results, or even sometimes to calculations giving whatever results are desired by the person doing the calculating. But almost any system used to score the 1936 Olympics will place Germany first, because of its many victories in the less-publicized sports, and the United States second, although American athletes swept the prestigious track and field events.

These results of the Berlin Olympics are clear enough, but what of the broader, longer-term results? Did Hitler score an outstanding propaganda victory? Or did the accomplishments of a handful of black American athletes spoil his propaganda?

Certainly much of the propaganda effort worked very well indeed. Visitors may have snickered when the dictator left hurriedly rather than stay to congratulate a black athlete, but they may still have been impressed by the neat, polished, well-organized aspects of German life that were emphasized in Berlin. It was easy to assume that Hitler, like some politicians in democratic countries, was a bit of a fool but that his followers were hardworking, honest people. (And it was one of the contradictions of the German character that in many ways Germans *were* hardworking, honest people and yet followed and supported the Nazis—a contradiction not as well known then as now, and one that caused many people to disbelieve the true nature of Nazi Germany.) Other visitors, noting the efficiency with which everything was done, the frequent presence of well-disciplined soldiers and sailors, and the occasional glimpses of aircraft and other military equipment, came to the conclusion that the Germans would be unbeatable in a war, and for that reason war with Germany should be avoided at any cost (or in other words, that Hitler should be given anything he wanted). Such visitors as were neither repelled nor amused by Hitler's personality were sometimes swept up in the German adulation of him. And the fact that Germany made the highest total Olympic score was certainly a propaganda coup.

The exploits of the black American athletes did not entirely blunt the Nazi propaganda effort. But if those athletes had not been there and had not won, that effort would have been complete; as it developed, the propaganda was considerably marred. Although such things are impossible to measure, it seems likely that because of the widely publicized black victories, more people remained skeptical about racial myths such as those of the Nazis than would otherwise have done so.

But even though the black victories did not stop the Nazis' precipitate rush into World War II, any more than Olympic propaganda ensured German victory once that war began, Owens, Woodruff, and their black colleagues accomplished something else. For the first time they brought to the attention of many other Americans in a dramatic way some of the capabilities of the black citizen. And for the first time other Americans, many perhaps grudgingly, felt proud of their black representatives.

Considering an even wider question, do the Olympics promote international sportsmanship? Certainly not always. When

The incomparable Jesse Owens, winner of four gold medals

the Peruvian soccer team lost to Austria in these 1936 games, the feeling in Peru ran so high that mobs attacked the German consulate in Lima—even though the Germans only provided the playing field and had nothing to do with the decision. During the 100-kilometer bicycle race at the Berlin velodrome—the specially built bicycle racetrack—there was a pileup of some twenty bicycles and riders, and during the ensuing fight the spectators nearly tore down the stands. Though in the Berlin Olympics there were many examples of good sportsmanship—Lutz Long's friendship with his strongest adversary, Jesse Owens, for example, or Ernest Harper's coaching of Kitei Son, his opponent in the marathon—there were at least as many examples of bitter competition. The Olympics may actually serve a greater purpose as outlets for international physical competition short of war than they do as occasions for international friendship.

Even that function may be getting out of hand. Hitler was the first to use the Olympic Games on a vast scale to further his political aims, but his manipulations seem almost amiable when compared to some of the things that have happened since, culminating in the political murders of Israeli athletes by Arab terrorists during the 1972 Olympics in Munich. Politics may in the end make it impossible to stage the Olympic Games at all. They can only be held if the world is willing to abide by rules—rules of general conduct between people as well as rules for particular sports. Whenever in this television age the attention of the whole world is focused for a time on a single group of competitors in a given place, the temptation for some people to use the event for their own political ends may now be too great. Only the future will tell.

Olympic Champions of the 1936 Berlin Games

TRACK AND FIELD (MEN)

100 m.	Owens (USA)	10.3 seconds
200 m.	Owens (USA)	20.7 "
400 m.	Williams (USA)	46.5 "
800 m.	Woodruff (USA)	1:52.9 minutes
1,500 m.	Lovelock (New Zealand)	3:47.8 "
5,000 m.	Höckert (Finland)	14:22.2 "
10,000 m.	Salminen (Finland)	30:15.4 "
Marathon	Son (Japan)	2:29:19.2 hours
110 m. hurdles	Towns (USA)	14.2 seconds
400 m. hurdles	Hardin (USA)	52.4 "
3,000 m. steeplechase	Iso-Hollo (Finland)	9:03.8 minutes
4 × 100 (400) m. relay	USA	39.8 seconds
4 × 400 (1,600) m. relay	Great Britain	3:09.0 minutes
50,000 m. walk	Whitlock (Great Britain)	4:30:41.4 hours
High jump	Johnson (USA)	6′7 7/8″
Broad (long) jump	Owens (USA)	26′5 21/64″
Pole vault	Meadows (USA)	14′3 1/4″
Triple jump (hop, skip, and jump)	Tajima (Japan)	52′6″
Shot put	Woellke (Germany)	53′1 13/16″
Javelin throw	Stöck (Germany)	235′8 1/2″
Discus throw	Carpenter (USA)	165′7 29/64″
Hammer throw	Hein (Germany)	185′4 1/16″
Decathlon	Morris (USA)	7,900 points *

* Old scoring system up to 1960

TRACK AND FIELD
(WOMEN)

100 m.	Stephens (USA)	11.5 seconds
80 m. hurdles	Valla (Italy)	11.7 ″
4 × 100 (400) m. relay	USA	46.9 ″
High jump	Csák (Hungary)	5′3″
Discus throw	Mauermayer (Germany)	156′3 1/4″
Javelin throw	Fleischer (Germany)	148′2 3/4″

SWIMMING
(MEN)

100 m. freestyle	Csik (Hungary)	57.6 seconds
400 m. freestyle	Medica (USA)	4:44.5 minutes
1,500 m. freestyle	Terada (Japan)	19:13.7 ″
100 m. backstroke	Kiefer (USA)	1:05.9 ″
200 m. breaststroke	Hamuro (Japan)	2:41.5 ″
4 × 200 (800) m. freestyle relay	Japan	8:51.5 ″
Springboard diving	Degener (USA)	163.57 points
Platform (high) diving	Wayne (USA)	113.58 ″

SWIMMING
(WOMEN)

100 m. freestyle	Mastenbroek (Netherlands)	1:05.9 minutes
400 m. freestyle	Mastenbroek (Netherlands)	5:26.4 ″
100 m. backstroke	Senff (Netherlands)	1:18.9 ″
200 m. breaststroke	Maehata (Japan)	3:03.6 ″
4 × 100 (400) m. freestyle relay	Netherlands	4:36.0 ″
Springboard diving	Gestring (USA)	89.27 points
Platform (high) diving	Poynton Hill (USA)	33.93 ″

ROWING

Single sculls	Schäfer (Germany)	8:21.5 minutes
Double sculls	Great Britain	7:20.8 "
Coxswainless pairs	Germany	8:16.1 "
Coxed pairs	Germany	8:36.9 "
Coxswainless fours	Germany	7:01.8 "
Coxed fours	Germany	7:16.2 "
Eights	USA	6:25.4 "

YACHTING

Star class	Germany
Monotype class	Netherlands
Six-meter class	Great Britain
Eight-meter class	Italy

CANOEING

Kayak singles	Hradetzky (Austria)	4:22.9
Kayak pairs	Austria	4:03.8
Canadian singles	Amyot (Canada)	5:32.1
Canadian pairs	Czechoslovakia	4:50.1

BOXING

Flyweight	Kaiser (Germany)
Bantamweight	Sergo (Italy)
Featherweight	Casanovas (Argentina)
Lightweight	Harangi (Hungary)
Welterweight	Suvio (Finland)
Middleweight	Despeaux (France)
Light heavyweight	Michelot (France)
Heavyweight	Runge (Germany)

CYCLING

1,000 m. time trial	van Vliet (Netherlands)	1:12.0 minutes
1,000 m. sprint	Merkens (Germany)	
2,000 tandem	Germany (Ihbe/Lorenz)	
4,000 m. team pursuit	France	4:45.0 minutes
Road race team	France	7:39:16.2 minutes
Road race	Charpentier (France)	

WRESTLING–GRECO-ROMAN

Flyweight	Lörincz (Hungary)
Bantamweight	Erkan (Turkey)
Lightweight	Koskela (Finland)
Welterweight	Svedberg (Sweden)
Middleweight	Johansson (Sweden)
Light heavyweight	Cadier (Sweden)
Heavyweight	Palusalu (Estonia)

WRESTLING–FREESTYLE

Bantamweight	Zombori (Hungary)
Featherweight	Pihlajamäki (Finland)
Lightweight	Karpati (Hungary)
Welterweight	Lewis (USA)
Middleweight	Poilve (France)
Light heavyweight	Fridell (Sweden)
Heavyweight	Palusalu (Estonia)

GYMNASTICS (MEN)

Combined exercises (team)	Germany	657.43 points
Combined exercises (individual)	Schwarzmann (Germany)	113.10 "
Horizontal bar	Saarvala (Finland)	19.36 "
Parallel bars	Frey (Germany)	19.07 "
Rings	Hudec (Czechoslovakia)	19.43 "
Floor exercises	Miez (Switzerland)	18.66 "
Pommeled horse	Frey (Germany)	19.33 "
Long horse vault	Schwarzmann (Germany)	19.20 "

GYMNASTICS (WOMEN)

Combined exercises (team)	Germany	506.50 points

WEIGHT LIFTING

Featherweight	Terlazzo (USA)	689 pounds
Lightweight	Mesbah (Egypt) and Fein (Austria)—tie	755 "
Middleweight	El Thouni (Egypt)	854 3/4 "
Light heavyweight	Hostin (France)	820 "
Heavyweight	Manger (Germany)	903 3/4 "

SHOOTING

Small-bore rifle (prone)	Rögeberg (Norway)	300 points
Free pistol	Ullman (Sweden)	559 "
Rapid-fire pistol	van Oyen (Germany)	36 "

FENCING

Individual foil (women)	Schacherer-Elek (Hungary)	6 wins
Team foil (men)	Italy	
Individual foil (men)	Gaudini (Italy)	7 "
Team épée	Italy	
Individual épée	Riccardi (Italy)	13 "
Team saber	Hungary	
Individual saber	Kabos (Hungary)	7 "

MODERN PENTATHLON

Individual	Handrick (Germany)	31.5 points

EQUESTRIAN

Three-day event (individual)	Stubbendorf (Germany)	362.30 points
Three-day event (team)	Germany	676.65 "
Dressage (individual)	Pollay (Germany)	352.00 "
Dressage (team)	Germany	5074 "
Grand Prix jumping (individual)	Hasse (Germany)	
Grand Prix jumping (team)	Germany	

TEAM SPORTS

Water polo	Hungary
Hockey	India
Basketball	USA
Football (soccer)	Italy

Bibliography

News reports of the period are the primary sources. In addition, the following volumes have been consulted.

Burden, Hamilton. *The Nuremberg Party Rallies: 1923–1939.* New York: Frederick A. Praeger, 1967.

Fromm, Bella. *Blood and Banquets: A Berlin Social Diary.* New York: Harper & Brothers, 1942.

Girardi, Wolfgang. *Olympic Games.* New York and Glasgow: International Library, 1972.

Johnson, William O., Jr. *All That Glitters Is Not Gold.* New York: G. P. Putnam's Sons, 1972.

Kieran, John, and Daley, Arthur. *The Story of the Olympic Games.* Rev. ed. Philadelphia: J. B. Lippincott Company, 1973.

Mandell, Richard D. *The Nazi Olympics.* New York: The Macmillan Company, 1971.

Owens, Jesse, and Neimark, Paul G. *Blackthink: My Life As Black Man and White Man.* New York: Morrow, 1970.

Shirer, William L. *Berlin Diary: The Journal of a Foreign Correspondent, 1934–1941.* New York: Knopf, 1941.

———. *The Rise and Fall of the Third Reich.* New York: Simon & Schuster, 1960.

Weyand, Alexander M. *The Olympic Pageant.* New York: The Macmillan Company, 1952.

Index

About the Author

James P. Barry, a 1940 graduate of Ohio State University (cum laude, with distinction, Phi Beta Kappa) has been a career army officer, a university administrator, and an editor. He fought in Europe, including Germany, during World War II, and since then has lived in Germany for several years. He has written a number of books and articles on historical subjects, including these titles in the Focus Books series: *The Louisiana Purchase, The Noble Experiment, The Battle of Lake Erie, Bloody Kansas,* and *Henry Ford and Mass Production. The Berlin Olympics* is his first book for the World Focus Books series. His most recent book is *Ships of the Great Lakes,* an illustrated history. Mr. Barry lives in Columbus, Ohio, and is married to a high school librarian.